This book is dedicated to Aline and
William "Bras De Fer"

The author of this book Benjamin James
Baillie lives and works in Normandy

The Last Prince

Wales' Braveheart: Owain Glyndwr, The last Welsh Prince of Wales 1359-1415 A.D

By
Benjamin James Baillie

Contents

Introduction
Wales 1283 – 1400 A.D
The Statute of Rhuddlan 1284 A.D
Rhys ap Maredudd, Lord of Deheubarth
Madog ap Llywelyn 1294-1295 A.D
Owain Glyndŵr, of noble Lineage
Loyal service to the crown
The seeds of rebellion 1400 A.D
The uprising, September 1400 A.D
Defeat; the Battle / Skirmish of Vyrnwy / Afon Erfynwy
The capture of Conwy castle 1401 A.D
The first Victory: the Battle of Mynydd Hyddgen
King Henry IV's second expedition into Wales 1401 A.D
The Battle of Tuthill, November 1401 A.D
1402 A.D The year of destiny
The Battle of Bryn Glas / Pilleth 22nd June 1402 A.D
The Anti-Welsh Penal laws 1402 A.D
War in the south 1402-1403 A.D
Prince Henry and the Battle of Shrewsbury 1403 A.D
The Battle of Stalling down 1403 A.D
1404 A.D "The Lord of all Wales"
France enters the war
The skirmishes of Campstone Hill and Craig Y Dorth, summer 1404 A.D
1405 A.D, The beginning of the end
The Tripartite indenture
The Battles of Grosmont and Pwll Melyn 1405 A.D
Last through of the dice "The French invasion"
1406 A.D The rebellion falters
1407A.D The fall of resistance, Aberystwyth castle
The winter of 1407-1408 A.D
The siege of Harlech 1408-1409 A.D
The last raid into England 1409 A.D
The fugitive and disappearance 1410 – 14 ? A.D

Owain Glyndŵr, Prince of Wales

Introduction

Owain Glyndŵr was the last native Welshman to hold the title Prince of Wales. After the Anglo-Norman conquest by the nation breaking King Edward I "Longshanks" in the late 13th century Wales was carved up between the English crown and the hated Marcher Lords. Its people were oppressed and treated like second class citizens within their own country. In 1400 A.D a little known Welsh nobleman by the name of Owain Glyndŵr rose up in rebellion and led the Welsh people into a brutal war for independence. For over a decade Wales' "Braveheart" stuck fear into the hearts of his enemies before disappearing like King Arthur into the mists and mountains of his beloved homeland never to be seen again.

Wales 1283 – 1400 A.D

The year 1283 A.D was a black year for Wales. Prince Llywelyn ap Gruffudd (the last) had been killed at the Battle of Irfon Bridge in December 1282 A.D. His brother Dafydd ap Gruffydd briefly proclaimed himself Prince of Wales, but by the summer of 1283 A.D he had been captured by men of his own tongue and handed over to the English for execution.

Memorial to Prince Llywelyn "the last" Abbey Cwmhi, Mid Wales

At Shrewsbury the Prince was put to death in a gruesome manner. Firstly he was tied to the tail of a horse and dragged through the streets towards his place of execution. He was then hanged by the neck, disemboweled and had his entrails burned in front of his eyes. Finally he was beheaded and quartered. His head was sent to London to rest beside Llywelyn's.

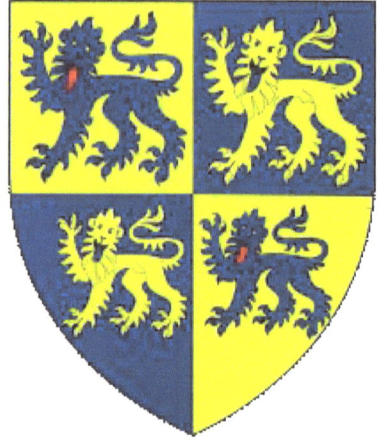

Arms of Dafydd ap Gruffydd

The Statute of Rhuddlan 1284 A.D

On the 19th of March 1284 A.D Edward I issued the statue of Rhuddlan, otherwise known as the statute of Wales. The statue set out how Wales would be governed and organised. The old Celtic Principalities were replaced with new English type Shires (Anglesey, Caernarfon, Flint, Merioneth Carmarthen, and Cardiganshire). Although English law was introduced, many of the old Welsh laws were retained. Edward bestowed the title Prince of Wales upon his infant son, Edward of Caernafon in 1301 A.D. The young Prince was born in the half built castle of Caernarfon on the 25th of April 1284 A.D. According to legend the Welsh had asked the King to give them a Prince who spoke Welsh. Edward I placed the baby on his shield and presented him to the people of Wales with the response I offer you a Prince who speaks no English at all.

Edward I was also in the progress of building "the iron ring" of monumental castles to cement his control over Wales. The castles of Conwy, Caernarfon, and Harlech were constructed to deter the Welsh from any thoughts of rebellion.

Rhys ap Maredudd, Lord of Deheubarth

The first test came in 1287 A.D when Rhys ap Maredudd (the native Welsh Lord of Deheubarth) revolted in South Wales. Rhys had submitted to Edward I back in 1277A.D during the first Welsh war. He had been promised Dinefwr which was the historic capital of Deheubarth, but Edward stalled on the deal. By 1287 A.D Rhy's feud with the Giffard Marcher lord of Llandovery exploded. Rhys took the sword and laid waste to the English settlements and castles in Deheubarth. Although Rhys succeeded in capturing Dinefwr and Carreg Cennen his success was short lived. Edward dispatched troops under the command of the Earl of Cornwall to deal with the rebellion.

Dryslwyn Castle, Dyfed (South Wales)

A huge royal army of 11,000 men assembled in Carmarthen and then laid siege the Rhy's castle at Dryslwyn. Huge trebuchet's battered the walls and the King's engineers dug mines beneath the foundations.

On the 5th of September the English captured the castle, but Rhys and his close family managed the escape. He remained at large until 1291 A.D when he was finally captured. Like Dafydd before him Rhys was taken over the border to England where he was executed at York.

Madog ap Llywelyn 1294-1295 A.D

In the autumn of 1294 A.D a more serious rebellion broke out in the Principality. The revolt was led by Madog ap Llywelyn, who was a direct descendant of Owain Gwynedd (Welsh Prince of Gwynedd) who had defied King Henry II "Plantagenet" in the 12th century. Madog was also distantly related to both Llywelyn (the last) and Dafydd ap Gruffydd. Natural resentment towards the English officials and representives had been smoldering since the subjugation, but the final straw was a tax of a fifteenth on movables. Madog proclaimed himself Prince of Wales and raised the standard of rebellion. The rebels quickly took control of the Island of Anglesey and then crossed the Meni straits and descended on the administrative heart of English control in Gwynedd, Caernarfon. In a surprise attack Madog's men overrun the defensive walls and entered the town. Once inside they went on the rampage and burned Caernafron to the ground. The castle which was not finished at the time was badly damaged. Edward's sheriff Roger de Pulesdon was murdered in the attack and the tax and exchequer records were gladly destroyed. By November nearly every English Castle in North Wales had either fallen or was being besieged. The situation required the presence of the King himself, who called off an expedition to France and marched north to confront the Welsh. In December the King advanced into Wales with a colossal army of over 30,000 men.

The Mighty castle of Caernafron was only partly built when it was attacked by Madog ap Llywelyn in 1294 A.D

The advanced vanguard was ambushed near Bangor and Edward had to seek protection behind the walls of Conwy castle. For over a week the Welsh beseiged Conwy and the King was forced to drink water mixed with honey until he was relieved by the main force of his army. It seemed that Wales was on the brink of overthowing English domination, but then disaster struck. Madog had ventured south, far from the saftey of the mountians of Snowdonia. Near Montgomery in the middle March of Wales his force was supprised by William de Beauchamp (the Earl of Warwick) at Maes Moydog. Madog's men fought bravely, but the Earl's use of combined archers and cavarly shattered the Welsh spearmen.

Although Madog escaped the carnage; his defeat was a major blow for Welsh independance. By the summer, Madog was captured and sent to the tower of London. Without a leader the revolt was crushed and Edward built more castles such as Beaumaris on Anglesey to tighten his control on the Principality. Although there were later rebellions in the 14th century, notably under Llywelyn Bren (Llywelyn of the Woods) and Owain Lawgoch, Wales was firmly in the grip of English domination

Owain Glyndŵr, of noble Lineage

It is not certain when or where Owain Glyndŵr was born, but it was sometime between 1349-1359 A.D. He may have either been conceived at the family fief of Sycharth, near Oswestry in the Welsh Marches or in Trefgarn (Pembrokeshire).

What is certain is that Owain was descended from the Royal houses of the ancient Kingdoms of Wales. His Father Gruffydd Fychan (the younger) was decended from Bleddyn ap Cynfyn (Prince of Powys). Through his mother Elen Goch, Owian was decended from Prince Rhys ap Tewdwr (Kingdom of Deheubarth). Elen was also a great-great grandaughter of Prince Llywelyn the last (Prince of Gwynedd and Wales). Owain's great-great grandfather (another Gruffydd Fychan) had fought for Llywelyn the last in the Welsh wars of 1277 and 1282-83 A.D. After the execution of Dafydd ap Gruffydd and the Anglo-Norman subjudgation of the Principality Gruffydd Fychan was prondoned upon the request of John de Warren (the Earl of Surrey). He was given the right to hold the fief of Glyndyfrdwy directly from the crown.

Loyal service to the crown

Like many Welshmen Owain's father served in the armies of Edward III and the Black Prince during the 100 hundred years war in France. Upon his father's death in 1370 A.D Owain inherited the estates of Glyndyfrdwy and Cynllaith. During his minority he was sent to Chirk castle and became a ward of the Marcher Lord Richard Fitz-Alan (the Earl of Arundel). He was educated and could speak Latin, Norman-French, English and his natural tongue Welsh. These skills allowed him to study law at the prestigious "Inns of court" in London. There he met Margaret Hanmer, the daughter of Sir David Hanmer, one of the Justices of King Richard II. After a few years of courting one another the happy couple were married in 1383 A.D.

Fitz-Alan coat of arms

After his apprenticeship in law Owain entered into the retinue of the Earl of Arundel for military service. He was placed under the command of the Welsh Captain Sir Degory Sais at Berwick upon Tweed on the border with Scotland. According to the Welsh bard Gruffydd Llwyd, Owain fought in Richard II's Scottish war. On one occasion he was unhorsed, but bravely drove off his attackers with nothing but a broken lance.

Gruffydd Llwyd:

"Owain fought and drove the Scots before him like goats"

Owain rose in promence and acompanied King Richard II to France in 1385 AD, gaining the positon as Royal shield bearer. Astute in law, Owain was called to give evidence at Chester court to settle a dispute between two knights (Sir Richard Scrope & Sir Robert Grosvenour) who bore the same coat of arms. Owain and his brother Tudor ap Gruffudd are both mentioned on the Earl's muster roll in 1387 A.D. He may have even fought against the King at the Battle of Radcot Bridge in the same year.

As England descended into near civil war between the increasingly tyrannical King Richard II and his opponents "the Lords appellant" Owain retired to Glyndyfrdwy to run the family fief. In 1397 Owain lost any influence at court on death of Earl Richard Fitz-Alan. The Earl was arrested and then executed by the King on charges of treason. Although Owain does not seem to have taken part in the rebellion and ousting of King Richard II by his cousin Henry Bolingbroke in 1399 A.D he certainly hoped for a new beginning on the accession of the new King Henry IV.

The seeds of rebellion 1400 A.D

One of the major powerbrokers in the Northern Marches of Wales was Reginald de Grey. In 1282 A.D the first Lord Grey was granted the new Marcher Lordship of Dyffryn Clwyd (Vale of Clwyd) by King Edward I. De Grey's powerbase was Ruthin castle and from there the family exercised considerable power across the Lordship. The origin of the rebellion was a small strip of land called Croesau (modernday Bryneglwys). The farmland lay between Owain's fief of Glyndyfrdwy and De Grey's Lordship of Ruthin to the north. De Grey claimed the land, but was unable to gain it during the reign of Richard II. Things changed under the new regime of Henry IV for De Grey was a close friend of the King and also a member of the Royal "Privy council". Sometime in early 1400 A.D De Grey's men took control of the common land by force. The peasant tenants were evicted, to which they remonstrated to their righful Lord: Owain Glyndŵr. Owain decided to go through the correct legal channels and bring his case before the spring parliament. The newly crowned King Henry IV sat uneasy upon the throne of England. Many regarded him as an usurper and saw the rightful heir to Richard II was a certain Roger De Mortimer (Earl of March). In such a precarious position Henry needed to appease the great magnates of the land including Reginald de Grey. When Owain's complaint was

Effigy of King Henry IV, Canterbury Cathedral

brought before Parliament it was dismissed without even being given a hearing. The Bishop of St Asaph (John Trefor) who had tried to mediate between Owain and De Grey was appalled by the decision and warned Parliament that such blatant injustices against the Welsh nobility would cause discontent and possible rebellion. The English nobles on hearing the Bishop's comments replied with the contemptuous remarks

"We care nothing for those bare footed scrubs"

The final straw came when King Henry IV summoned the nobility of the Kingdom for a campaign against England's Northern neighbour: Scotland. De Grey was responsible for sending out the commissions of array in the Northern Marches. He deliberately delayed summoning Owain, thus when Owain failed to turn up he could accuse the Welshman of being a traitor to the crown. Henry at once declared Owain a traitor and ordered De Grey to seize Owain and his lands.

De Grey hatched a plan which would have been worthy of the most unscrupulous Marcher Lord of them all, William De Broase (the Lord of Abergavenny) to capture Glyndŵr. According to the Mostyn manuscript De Grey invited Owain to a peace conference so he could be reconciled. Owain agreed, but on the condition that De Grey be accompanied by no more than a handful of his retinue. De Grey secretly ordered a large force of soldiers to shadow his unarmed force and strike once the rendezvous place had been discovered. Owain was by no means willing to walk into a trap on the word of his untrustworthy neighbour. He positioned his bard Iolo Goch nearby to watch out for any suspicious activity. While De Grey and Owain dined together Iolo spotted De Grey's troops approaching the vicinity. Iolo at once returned to the hall and started to sing a song in Welsh, knowing that De Grey could not understand. It was code, telling Owain that De Grey's men were approaching. Owain releasing it was a trap excused himself and quickly escaped the hall retreating into the darkness. A declared traitor and a hunted man, Owain decided that the only course of action left open to him was to rise up and revolt. He ordered word to be sent out to his family, friends and the local Welsh population to meet him at Glyndyfrdwy.

Glyndŵr's mound / castle, Glyndyfrdwy, Wales

The uprising, September 1400 A.D

On the 16th of September 1400 A.D at Owain's chief seat of Glyndyfrdwy the standard of rebellion was officially raised. As well as his son Gruffydd, those present included his brother Tudur, members of his wife's family (the Hanmers) John Aswick, Ieuan Fychan of Moeliwrch and Hywel ap Madoc Kyffin (the Dean of St Asaph). On that fateful day they proclaimed Owain Prince of Wales and swore to make Wales free of English domination.

The rebels decided their first target was to be none other than the centre of hatred: De Grey's Marcher capital of Ruthin. In the nearby forest of Coed Marchon Owain's men gathered and prepared to strike Ruthin on St Matthews's day. As dawn broke on the 21st of September the Welsh partisans slowly entered the walled town mingling with the traders and visitors. As the last group made their way in, Owain gave the signal to unleash hell. The town guards were caught completely by surprise and quickly overwhelmed in the initial fighting. The houses and shops were set on fire and anyone who resisted was put to the sword. The castle where De Grey normally resided (De Grey was absent at the time) managed to close the gates just before the Welsh could enter it. Owain contented himself with ransacking nearly every building within the town walls. The Welsh departed, leaving Ruthin a smouldering heap of ruins and headed north towards Denbigh.

Ruins of the gatehouse of Denbigh castle. (North east Wales)

Owain's growing war band descended upon the market town of Denbigh and burned it to the ground. Within less than a week the whole of North east Wales was in total chaos, the great Edwardian castles of Flint, Rhuddlan, Harwarden and Holt were all besieged. Unable to take the castles without heavy siege machines Owain decided to head south and raise rebellion in the middle March of Wales.

Defeat; the Battle / Skirmish of Vyrnwy / Afon Erfynwy

Oswestry was taken with the help of some local Welshmen who decided to join the revolt. They then attacked Powis castle and sacked the important border town of Welshpool. On September 26th 1400 A.D at the battle/skirmish of the river Vyrnwy / Afon Erfynwy Owain's army was surprised by a hastily gathered force of Englishmen under the command of Sir Hugh Burnell (the Governor of Bridgenorth Castle). Hugh attacked Owain's army and put them to flight. It was a shattering defeat, but Owain managed to escape and avoid capture. Undeterred by the defeat Owain took shelter in the safety of the Berwyn Mountains and planned his next move.

On hearing the news from Wales King Henry IV gathered together the feudal host of England at Shrewsbury in late September and marched into Wales. After relieving the besieged castles of North Eastern Wales, the King advanced into Gwynedd and crossed the Menai straights to put down an insurrection by Owain's cousins (Rhys and Gwilyn ap Tudor) on Anglesey. Near Beaumaris the Royal party was attacked, forcing the King to seek refuge behind the walls of Beaumaris castle. Once the rebels had been driven off, Henry set about pacifying the island. In a revengeful attack he burned down the Franciscan abbey of Llanfraes. Unable the capture the Tudor brother's Henry returned to the mainland. The onset of winter forced the King to abandon the campaign and head back towards the border. He left Sir Henry Percy "Hotspur" as Justiciar of North Wales to contain the volatile situation

The capture of Conwy castle 1401 A.D

With no sign of Owain and no further insurrections against Royal authority it seemed that by the spring of 1401 A.D the rebellion was over. Owain's cousins Rhys and Gwilyn ap Tudor heard that the garrison of Conwy castle was undermanned and reduced to only 15 men-at-arms and 60 archers. Together they hatched a daring plan to capture the castle by guile during the Easter festivities. On the 1st of April (Good Friday) while the garrison and its commander Sir John Massy were in Church celebrating mass the rebels struck. One of Tudor's men disguised as a carpenter managed to gain access inside the castle. As the gate opened, Gwilyn and some 40 men overpowered the guards and took control of the impregnable fortress.

Conwy Castle, North Wales

The English commander was in complete shock and had to report the disastrous news to Sir Henry Precy "Hotspur" (Justiciar of North Wales) who was overseeing the re-building of Denbigh. At once Percy along with the King's son Prince Henry (later King Henry V) 120 men-at-arms and 300 archers rode directly to Conwy to assess the situation. On arriving at Conwy Percy realised there was no way he could re-take the castle by force, instead he besieged it hoping to starve the Welsh into submission.

The first Victory: the Battle of Mynydd Hyddgen

When the news reached Owain about his cousin's capture of one of the mightiest castles in medieval Europe he was overjoyed. The Tudors had taken the initiative in the North and now Owain needed to force home a victory in mid-Wales to open up the road to the south. During the winter Owain had been forging weapons and training his men ready for the fore-coming campaign at his mountain headquarters near the foot of Plynlimon (Cambrian Mountains). In June 1401 A.D a force of some 1,500 English and Flemish settlers from Cededigion and the Marcher Lordship of Pembrokeshire had been sent to crush rebel activity in the Plynlimon area. Owain and his 400 followers were severely outnumbered, but he used his military experience to lure the English deep into the boggy inhospitable terrain. The battle took place in the valley at a place called Esgair Ffordd (Ridgeway) where the Llygant and Nant Goch streams flow into the Hyddgen river. In the marshy ground the English infantry and armoured knights got bogged down. The lightly armoured Welsh used their hill ponies to increase mobility and inflict devastating loses upon the enemy with the deadly Welsh longbow. After a bloody climax to the battle, the English broke ranks and fled the field in total disarray.

Gruffudd Hiraethog "The Annals of Owen Glyndwr" reported:

"In the summer of 1401 Owain rose with 120 reckless men and robbers and took them to the uplands of Ceredingion. 1,500 men from the lowlands of Ceredigion, Rhos and Penfro assembled and came to the mountain to seize Owain. The battle was on Hyddgant Mountain and no sooner did the English soldiers turn their backs in flight than 200 of them were slain. Owain won great fame, and a large number of fighting men from all over Wales rose and joined him."

The battle of Mynydd Hyddgen was the first victory for Owain against an organised army. Overnight his reputation was transformed from a local rebel to a national leader against English oppression. Even in England Welsh workmen and scholars downed their tools, packed up their belongings and returned to Wales to join the fight for freedom.

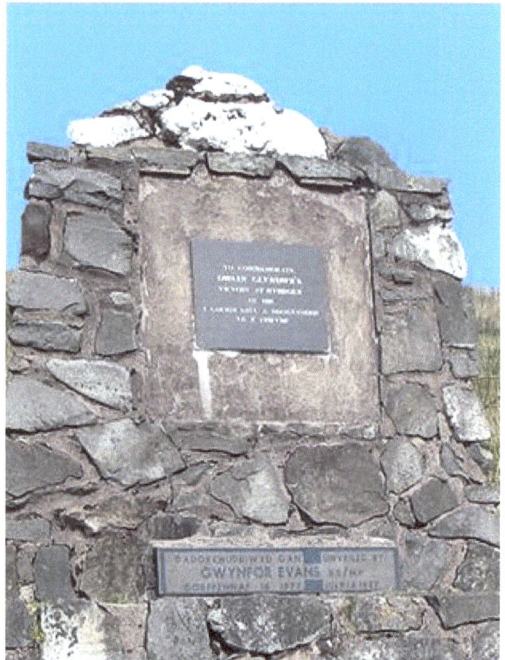

Memorial stone commemorating the Battle of Mynydd Hyddgen

Back in North Wales, after holding out for three months Owains cousins' negotiated the surrender of Conwy castle. On midsummer's day the Welsh garrison marched out of the castle unmolested. They handed over the keys, 1000

Marks and nine hostages as agreed in the terms of the surrender to Hotspur and Prince Henry.

This was one of the few chivalric acts honoured by both sides during the course of the war. With the castle back in English hands, Hotspur headed for Dolgelleu to try and force Owain into a pitched battle. Near the foot of Cader Idris the two forces skirmished, but neither side could claim victory.

King Henry IV's second expedition into Wales 1401 A.D

By September King Henry IV had little choice but to personally lead the English army into Wales and try and capture or kill Glyndŵr. In a three pronged attack the King's armies advanced from Hereford, Chester and Shrewsbury. When the Royal army reached Llandovery a local Welsh Lord by the name of Llywelyn ap Gruffydd Fychan offered to lead the English to Glyndŵr's whereabouts. Llywelyn was no traitor and he purposely led the English in the wrong direction, allowing Owain to escape. When the English realised they had been mislead by deception, Llywelyn was arrested and taken back to Llandovery to face the wrath of the King. Henry was furious and ordered Llywelyn to be executed in the market place. He was publicly hung, drawn and he had his entrails ripped out and burnt in front of his eyes. Finally he was quartered to serve as a warning to any more would-be traitors. The next target of the King's vengeance was the great Abbey of Strata Florida. Henry decided to use the abbey as a base to terrorise the local population. He accused the monks of conspiring with Owain and ejected them from the abbey grounds. To add further insult to injury he stabbled his horses at the high altar.

Overleaf: The battle of Mynydd Hyddgen→

The Chronicle of Adam of Usk:

"Owen Glyndwr continually attacked the English living in these parts and for that reason the English invaded. They ravaged and burned the area, sparing neither woman nor child, and they even destroyed Strata Florida where the King was staying. – The church desecrated and the high altar was converted into a stable. Henry IV later ordered reparations to the abbey, blaming the Welsh and his own men for the destruction."

Owain refused to fight a pitched battle against the superior forces of the King. Instead he disappeared back into the mountains conducting a guerilla campaign against the English. With the onset of winter Henry was forced yet again to abandon the search for Glyndŵr. On his way back towards the English border the notorious Welsh weather reeked havoc upon the King's retreating army. Roads and tracks were washed away and many of the superstitious English soldiers believed that Owain was a magician and was to blame for their torment.

The Battle of Tuthill, November 1401 A.D

Free from interference from the main English force that had retreated back to England, Owain rode north into Gwynedd. On the 2nd of November his force descended out of the mists of the Snowdonia Mountains and attacked Caernarfon. Overlooking the town on Twt Hill Owain's standard bearer Elis ap Rhisiart unveiled the sacred gold Dragon banner on a white background (Baner y Ddraig Aur). The Dragon banner was steeped in Welsh legend and heralded back to the time of King Arthur and Uthr Pendragon. By using this symbol Owain was in effect proclaiming himself to be the

"Meibion Darogan" (son of the Prophecy) from Welsh mythology, who would free Wales from subjugation.

The battle for Caernafron was a bloody affair with some 200 Welsh left dead after the attack. Although Glyndŵr failed to capture the castle, the audacity of the raid highlighted the fact that Owain could strike at any town or castle in Wales at will.

Baner y Ddraig Aur / Golden Dragon banner

1402 A.D The year of destiny

Owain decided to concentrate his campaign of 1402 A.D in the Marches of Wales. According to the Peniarth Manuscript in April 1402 A.D Owain surrounded and besieged Ruthin again. On this occasion Lord De Grey was inside the castle, after his men repulsed the Welsh attack De Grey spotted the banner of Glyndŵr himself a few hundred meters from the castle walls. Unable to resist the chance of capturing Glyndŵr, De Grey led a reckless charge with his household knights. Owain had been expecting such an act of bravado, and as the English knights charged towards him he quickly wheeled around his horse and led De Grey and his men into a deadly ambush. In the forest of Coed Marchan De Grey's force suddenly halted their charge when they spotted a large force in front of them in the distance. However, it was a Welsh ruse as the supposedly large force was nothing more than captured cloaks and helmets set on poles. De Grey ordered his men to retreat back towards Ruthin, but it was too late. Glyndŵr's men descended from out of the forest and began pulling the English knights from their horses and hacking them to death. De Grey and six of his close companions managed to escape the carnage and make their way to Bryn Saith Marchog (Hill of the seven knights).

Within a short time De Grey and the 6 surviving knights of his household were surrounded and taken prisoner. Owain decided against killing the English Marcher Lord who had caused the rebellion and instead held him for ransom. De Grey was carted off to the prison at Llansanffraid. He was later transferred to the safety of Dolbadarn castle in the heart of the Snowdonia Mountains.

After De Grey's capture Glyndŵr attacked the Middle March which brought him into direct conflict with the border's most powerful and illustrious family "the Mortimer's".

Originally from Normandy the Mortimer's came to England after the Norman Conquest. They rose in prominence over the next 350 years and by 1330 A.D Roger De Mortimer was granted the title "Earl of March". The Earl of March at the time of Owain's rebellion was Edmund (IV) De Mortimer, who was only 8 years of age.

De Mortimer coat of arms, St Laurence church, Ludlow

As well as being the Earl of March, Edmund was also the heir to the deposed King Richard II. For that reason the boy and his brother had been taken into custody by Henry IV. The vast Mortimer estates were controlled by the Earl's Uncle Sir Edmund Mortimer, who also had a claim to the English throne far greater than that of Henry IV.

Glyndŵr's marauding army ravaged the Mortimer Lordship of Radnorshire. In a scorched earth policy even the great Abbey Cwmhir was partially burned. Coincidently Abbey Cwmhir is believed to be the final resting place of the headless corpse of Llywelyn "the last" (The last Prince of Wales).

Wigmore castle, Herefordshire, ancestral home of the Mortimers

The Battle of Bryn Glas / Pilleth 22nd June 1402 A.D

By June Glyndŵr's men were within striking distance of Wigmore castle (the ancestral home of the Mortimers).

Sir Edmund Mortimer raised an army from the Mortimer fiefs of North Herefordshire and Maelienydd to combat the Welsh menace. Some 1,500-2,000 Marcher troops mustered at Ludlow castle and marched out over the Dinham Bridge towards Wales.

Mortimer's scouts reported that Glyndŵr's troops were in the vicinity of the Lugg valley between Knighton and Presteigne. After ransacking Knighton, Knucklas and many of the surrounding villages Glyndŵr and his trusted lieutenant Rhys Gethin decided to make a stand at Pilleth/Bryn Glas. Although outnumbered 2:1 Owain used the terrain just as he had done at the Battle of Mynydd Hyddgen. He positioned his main force on the hill (Bryn Glas / Green hill) above the village. The steep gradient allowed him to mask many of his soldiers from the view of the advancing English army.

Glyndŵr sent in his lightly armed skirmishers to attack to English vanguard. Mortimer's men took the bait and committed themselves into a frontal assault and charged after the Welsh troops up the sloop of the hill. When they were within distance, Owain ordered his longbow men to release a barrage of deadly arrows into the English ranks. Once the English line had been softened up, Glyndŵr's main force used the momentum of the hill and charged into the disintegrating English front line. At this very moment: the Welsh archers from Maelienydd and Radnorshire in Mortimer's army defected.

Instead of attacking their fellow Welshmen, they loosed their arrows into the backs of the English troops. Attacked from both front and behind the English army was cut to pieces in the savage hand to hand combat. Sir Walter Devereaux of Weobley and Henry IV's Knight- Marshal Robert Whitney were both slain in the fighting.

Sir Edmund Mortimer (Battle of Bryn Glas / Pilleth)

Only the English commander Edmund Mortimer and Sir John Clanvowe were taken alive as the battle turned into a rout. The entire Mortimer army had been slaughtered with only a few survivors managing to make it back across the border to safety. According to the Chronica Majora by Thomas Walshingham after the battle the Welsh women mutilated the corpses of the English dead.

"The Welsh women cut off the genitalia of the English dead. They put the member of each dead man into his mouth, and hung the testicles from his chin. They also cut off their noses and put them into their arses. They also refused to allow the bodies to be buried and commended to God"

The site of the Battle of Pilleth / Bryn Glas 22nd June 1403 A.D

With nothing to stop them: the victorious Welsh army crossed the border and sacked the market town of Leominster.

Mortimer was held in the town's gaol, while Glyndŵr's men plundered the Priory church. Although only 12 miles away, Owain decided against attacking the great border town of Hereford and instead returned back to Wales with his valuable prisoner. King Henry received the disastrous news from Pilleth and also a letter from the burgers of Hereford urging him to come at once before all was lost. The King sent letters instructing the Barons of the Welsh-March to fortify their castles and prepare for war. He also sent Sir Hugh Burnell (who had defeated Owain near Welshpool in 1400 A.D) to restore order and check Owain's advance in the borderlands. Hugh immediately strengthened and re-garrisoned the Norman castles of Montgomery, Cefnllys and Dolforwyn.

Arms of King Henry IV

In late summer King Henry IV arrived in Hereford and prepared for a third invasion of Wales. Just as before in the two previous campaigns the Welsh weather broke. Torrential rain battered the Royal armies and when the Seven, Wye and Dee rivers broke their banks, supplying the troops became near impossible. Henry was frustrated, but had little choice to abandon the campaign.

The Annales Henrici Quarti:
"Glyndwr, almost destroyed the King and his armies, by magic as it was thought, for from the time they entered Wales to the time they left, never did a gentle air breathe on them, but throughout whole days and nights, rain mixed with snow and hail afflicted them with cold beyond endurance.

←The capture of Sir Edmund Mortimer by the Welsh, aided by his own archers

The Anti-Welsh Penal laws 1402 A.D

Back in England King Henry IV summoned Parliament to discuss to volatile situation in Wales. Instead of issuing a pardon to the rebels and restoring Owain his lands, the King decided to pass a series of draconian anti-Welsh laws.

No Welshman was allowed to hold an official post.

It was illegal for any Englishman to be prosecuted in Wales by a Welshman.

Bards were forbidden to sustain themselves by minstrelsy.

Welshmen were not allowed to carry weapons without an official licence.

All garrisons and walled towns were to be manned by Englishmen.

No Englishman, if he was married to a Welsh woman, was allowed to hold an official post in Wales or the Marches.

No Welshmen unless he was a Lord or Bishop, could possess a castle of fortified house.

Welshmen were forbidden to hold any meetings without a crown representative present.

By issuing these laws Henry hoped to cower the Welsh people into submission, it however had the reverse effect. Welshmen and women flocked to Glyndŵr's banner and joined the revolt.

Winter 1402 A.D

Not all Welshmen were sympathic to Owain's cause, the Welsh Lord of Nannau, Hywel Sele (Owain's distant cousin) was an active supporter of the English crown. Glyndŵr captured him, but he was ambushed by Hywel's supporters near Dolgelleu. Owain and his men had to fight there way over the Llanelltyd Bridge, leaving over 60 of their pursuers dead. Although Hywel agreed to support Glyndŵr after prolonged negotiation, he secretly planned to assassinate him. While the two were together hunting deer, Hywel aimed his bow at Owain and fired! The deadly arrow embedded itself into Owain's clothing, but was stopped by Glyndŵr's concealed shirt of mail.

Owain in a fit of rage immediately slew Hywel on the spot. He threw Hywel's corpse into the hollow trunk of an old oak tree (called Derwen Ceubren yr Ellyll / the Hollow Tree of the Demons) where legend says in rested undiscovered for the next 40 years.

With the King back in England, Glyndŵr continued his reign of terror in the middle March. He stormed the town and castle of New Radnor. In a gruesome act of retribution he ordered 60 men from the captured garrison to be decapitated. Their bodies were then hung from the curtain walls to put fear into the hearts of his enemies. During the winter of 1402 A.D the negotiations for the release of Owain's highly valuable prisoner Lord Grey were completed.

The price for De Grey's release had been set at 10,000 marks, 6,000 of which was to be paid on the 6th of November (Martinmas). De Grey's eldest son was kept hostage until the remainder of the ransom could be raised. The King decided not to pay the ransom for Glyndŵr's other prisoner, Edmund Mortimer. Henry may have been glad to have seen a rival claimant to the throne captured and hoped Glyndŵr would dispose of him.

His plan backfired and Mortimer defected and joined the Welsh rebellion. Mortimer also had royal Welsh blood running through his veins for his ancestor Ralph II had married Gwladus Du (a daughter of Prince Llywelyn the Great). To seal the pact with Glyndŵr, Edmund married Owain's daughter Catrin in November. He then wrote a series of letters to his tenants in the Marches of Wales proclaiming that Henry was nothing more than a usurper and if Richard II was still alive he should be restored to the throne. Knowing full well that Richard II was indeed dead, Edmund was angling the crown for his nephew (Edmund IV, the Earl of March).

War in the south 1402-1403 A.D

South Wales and the southern Marches was Glyndŵr's next target. Nowhere was save from Owain's children (this was the name given to Glyndŵr's maundering armies).

The Chronicle of Adam of Usk:

"Like a second Assyrian, the rod of God's anger, he did deeds of unheard cruelty with fire and sword"

As the Welsh broke out into the South, the English border castles were put to the ultimate test. Usk was burnt to the

Ground and Glyndŵr's men took the stone keep at Caerleon. The castle garrison of Abergavenny watched helplessly as the Owain's "children" destroyed the town. Monmouthshire was King Henry's personal power block, being part of the Duchy of Lancaster. Henry's son the future Henry V was born in the great hall of Monmouth castle and the King also held several heraldic titles in the region. The Lancastrian castles of Grosmont, Tretower, Skenfrith and White (Llantilio) put up stout defences and held out against Owain's direct assaults.

Castle house, (Current HQ of the Royal Monmouthshire Royal Engineers Militia) built on the site of the great stone tower of Monmouth castle

By the summer of 1403 A.D the Royalist stronghold of Carmarthen was under siege. The castle's constable unable to resist the rebel attacks any longer surrendered the mighty fortress and handed over the keys to Glyndŵr himself.

After the capture of Carmarthen Royal authority collapsed in South Wales. Only a few diehard castles held out including the famous Norman bastion of Kidwelly. Glyndŵr's men aided by a naval contingent of French and Breton pirates broke through Kidwelly's defences and ransacked the town. The great gatehouse was badly damaged, but the castle garrison managed the thwart off the attackers and hold out until they were relieved later in the year. Owain's supporters then marched into Pembrokeshire, intent on capturing the mighty castle of Pembroke and its important harbour. Pembroke castle had been the home

The great keep of Pembroke castle built by Sir William Marshal

of the legendary knight Sir William Marshal and was also the gateway to the English colony of Ireland. Sir Thomas (Lord Carew) had been charged with defending the shire against the advancing Welsh onslaught. Using his local knowledge, he managed to annihilate some 800 men of Owain's advance column on route to Pembroke.

Prince Henry and the Battle of Shrewsbury 1403 A.D

Prince Henry now 16 years of age was given his first real military command in Wales. One of the Prince's first acts was the destruction of Owain's fortified house/castle at Sycharth and his ancestral seat of Glyndyfrdwy. The Prince marched into Merionethshire and wasted the land with fire and sword, but within a few weeks he was forced to withdraw and disband his force because of insufficient funds to pay his men.

The Prince was not the only noble waiting to receive money from the crown; the Percy's had a much larger axe to grind with over 20,000 pounds of debts dating back to 1399 A.D. The Percy's had been instrumental in bringing Henry IV to power and supporting the Lancastrian cause, but by the summer of 1403 A.D they had decided to revolt. There were a number of disagreements and grievances between themselves and the King, principally the ransom money for the Scottish prisoners captured at the Battle of Homildon Hill and the refusal to pay Sir Edmund Mortimer's ransom (Sir Henry Percy "Hotspur" was linked by marriage to Edmund's sister Elisabeth Mortimer).

In early July Hotspur and some 200 retainers, including the Scottish Lord Archibald Douglas, 4th Earl of Douglas (his former prisoner) marched south from Northumberland and headed for Cheshire. The county had been staunchly loyal to the previous King Richard II. Hotspur hoped to use this support and also his influence within the region to recruit an army. With sufficient numbers flocking to the rebel banner at Chester, Hotspur decided to launch a daring plan to try and capture Prince Henry at Shrewsbury. Once the Prince would be in rebel hands he would cross the river Seven into Wales and link up with the forces of Owain Glyndŵr and Edmund Mortimer.

King Henry IV was at Nottingham when the news reached him that the Percys were in open revolt. By the time the King arrived at Burton upon Trent he became fully aware of the rebel plot to capture Prince Henry and join up with Glyndŵr's forces in Wales. After summoning commissions of array, Henry advanced to intercept Hotspur's forces who were also advancing on Shrewsbury. On the 20th of July 1403 Hotspur's men arrived outside Shrewsbury and were preparing to assault the town when the Royal banners of Henry IV were spotted converging on the town. In the evening the King ordered the Royal forces to ford the river Seven and form up into battle array near the Haughmond Abbey, blocking the rebel way into Wales. On Saturday 21st of July 1403 the two armies squared up to one another. Envoy's were sent from both camps to try and reach a peaceful settlement, but Hotspur's uncle Thomas Percy (the Earl of Worcester) declined the King's terms and encouraged his nephew to commit to battle . With the negotiations at an end the King ordered the Royal forces to advance towards the rebel position. When the Royal vanguard commanded by the Earl of Stafford came into range of Hotspur's archers, Henry Percy ordered his men let loose a deadly barrage of arrows.

One chronicler Thomas Walshingham reported that:
"The Royal vanguard fell like apples off a tree in the autumn, stirred up by a south-westerly wind"

The Earl of Stafford was probably killed in the initial archery duel. His men suffering from heavy casualties began to lost heart and flee the battle. On seeing this retreat Hotspur launched a mounted cavalry charge against the Kings division.

The King's standard bearer Sir James Blount was killed and the Royal standard was overthrown. Several times Hotspur's men thought they had killed the King himself, but Henry had deployed decoys dressed in Royal livery to confuse the enemy.

As the two armies interlocked in the mêlée of the vicious hand to hand combat Prince Henry's rearguard division entered the fray. The Prince was struck in the face by an arrow, but he continued to lead the attack that was now enveloping the rebel forces.

The decisive moment came when according to one chronicler Hotspur raised the visor of his helmet and was struck in the face by an arrow, killing him instantly.

Statue of Sir Henry Percy "Hotspur" Alnwick

Other sources report that he was hacked to death in the thickest press of the battle. With Hotspur dead, many of his men began to look for a way off the bloody field. The Earl of Worcester and Archibald Douglas were captured and the overwhelming numbers of the King's forces finally won the day.

Shrewsbury had been a bloody encounter with several thousand dead and wounded littering the battlefield. Its consequences would also have far reaching effects for Owain Glyndŵr who was in South Wales when he heard the news of the defeat of his ally Henry "Hotspur" Percy.

The Battle of Stalling down 1403 A.D

Fresh from victory at the Battle of Shrewsbury King Henry turned his attention towards crushing Owain Glyndŵr and the Welsh revolt. His armies launched a devastating attack from Hereford into Wales. Although Carmarthen castle was recaptured from the Welsh, the King was unable to find or bring Owain Glyndŵr to battle.

After another fruitless campaign he returned to England and left the Earl of Arundel in charge of North Wales. The Duke of York and Richard Beauchamp (the Earl of Warwick) were to continue the struggle against the Welsh rebels in the south of the Principality.

In the autumn of 1403 A.D Owain's forces clashed with those of Henry IV at the Battle of Stalling Down, near the town of Cowbridge in Glamorgan. Although no great details are recorded of the battle, it seems that the English army was attacked or ambushed somewhere on the old Roman road today known as Bryn Owain (Owain's hill). The heaviest fighting took place in the deep valley called Pant-y Wenal. Owain and Cadwgan (Lord of Glyn) led from the front and inflicted horrendous casualties upon the King's men. Cadwagan hacked through the English ranks using a huge battle axe and was later nick-named "Cadwagan of the bloody axe". The fighting lasted for 18 hours, and it is said that the blood was up the fetlocks of the horses. The surviving English soldiers fled the battlefield and made their way to the safety of Cardiff.

In North Wales Caernarfon was besieged by a French fleet under the command of Jean d'Espagne. The castle garrison of only 28 men put up a heroic defence and prevented the great fortress from falling into Franco-Welsh hands.

1404 A.D "The Lord of all Wales"

On Anglesey the King's sheriff Maredudd ap Cynwrig and his escort were ambushed and virtually annihilated. This action caused Royal authority to collapse on the straticgally important island. With only a few major castles, notably Caernafron, Beaumarais, Aberystwyth, Conwy, Carreg Cennen and Harlech in English hands Owain decided to concentrate his resources on reducing these isolated outposts. Lying on the edge of Snowdonia Aberystwyth, Criccieth and Harlech were besieged by Glyndŵr's supporters with assistance from the French and Breton fleet.

Arms of Owain Glyndŵr

Cut off from supplies from the sea Criccieth was the first to fall. All hope was lost when a messenger from the castle was captured trying to get help from Conwy castle. Glyndŵr's men sacked the town and burnt the castle of the ground. Even today traces of burning can still be seen on the stones of the Leburn tower. Next to fall was the great Edwardian castle's of Aberystwyth and Harlech. The siege of Harlech lasted several months and even though the Castellan wanted to surrender, a few diehards resisted and held prisoner the would-be capitulators. Reduced to some 21 fighting men the garrison finally agreed to surrender in the spring of 1404 A.D. Harlech became Owain's principal place of residence. His wife, family and Edmund Mortimer all moved into the formidable fortress.

Harlech castle, North Wales

With most of Wales free from English oppression, Owain set out the vision for the future of Wales. He summoned a parliament at Machynlleth in central Wales. Most of the Welsh nobility and Clergy attended the parliament including representatives from France, Scotland and Castile. In an elaborate ceremony Owain Glyndŵr was crowned Prince of Wales. This was the greatest moment in the rebellion thus far and a high watermark of Owain's achievements. For the first time in over 120 years a Welshman could truly call himself Prince of Wales.

France enters the war

In May 1404 A.D Owain sent John Hanmer and his trusted friend Gruffydd Yonger as ambassadors to the French court of Charles VI. France had been with war with England on and off since the beginning the 14th century, (the 100 hundred years war). When Owain's ambassadors arrived

King Charles VI of France (le fou / the mad)

in Paris they were welcomed as friends with the same common enemy "England". The Government of Charles IV was eager to open up a second front and bring the war to England. By July 1404 A.D a formal treaty was concluded. The French agreed to send Glyndŵr some 3000 men under the command of the Marshal of France, Jean de Rieux. In the summer of 1404 A.D a French fleet under the command of Jacques de Bourbon (Le compte de la Marche) attacked the southern counties of England. Plymouth was sacked and by the end of 1404 A.D nowhere along the English coast was safe from attack.

The skirmishes of Campstone Hill and Craig Y Dorth, summer 1404 A.D

Owain and his trusted lieutenant Rhys Gethin harassed the English border extracting protection money from the communities unable to defend themselves. His raiding caught the attention of a young Knight, Richard Beauchamp (the Earl of Warwick). The Earl who had been fortifying the Norman castle of Brecon immediately advanced into Monmouthshire and caught up with the Welsh near Tretower. Elis ap Rhisiart was killed in the fighting and Owain's Standard the "Baner y Ddraig Aur" was captured by the English. Owain was lucky not to have been captured in the fray, but he quickly regrouped his men in the thickly wooded valleys and counter attacked Beauchamp's advancing troops. The Earl's men became overconfident and attacked a much larger Welsh force at Craig Y Dorth, just outside Monmouth. Unable to use their armoured cavalry in the difficult terrain they were defeated and forced to flee back to the safety of Monmouth.

Effigy of Sir Richard de Beauchamp, The Earl of Warwick

1405 A.D, The beginning of the end

During the winter of 1404 A.D an audacious plot was hatched by Constance of York (Countess of Gloucester) to free the young Earl of March (Edmund Mortimer) and his brother Roger. They would then be brought to Wales to join the rebellion with their Uncle Sir Edmund Mortimer and Owain Glyndŵr. Constance had her own axe to grind with Henry IV, for he had executed her husband Thomas le Despenser in 1400 A.D for his participation in the "Epiphany Rising". Constance managed to abduct the two young boys from Windsor castle and secretly travel across England towards Wales. Within striking distance of the Welsh Border near Cheltenham Constance and the Mortimer heirs were recaptured.

The Tripartite indenture

Although King Henry IV's men had foiled the plot to bring the Mortimer heirs into the hands of Owain Glyndŵr, a further coup d'etat was concluded between Glyndŵr, Mortimer and the Earl of Northumberland, Sir Henry Percy (the father of Hotspur who was killed at the Battle of Shrewsbury). The plan to remove Henry from the throne of England was called the tripartite indenture. At the home of the Dean of Bangor in remote North Wales Sir Thomas Bardolf signed the treaty on the behalf of the Earl of Northumberland. England would be spilt in two. All the counties north of the river Trent would be given to Henry Percy. The Midlands and the south of the country would be under the control of Edmund Mortimer and Wales would once again become an independent nation with Owain Glyndŵr as its Prince.

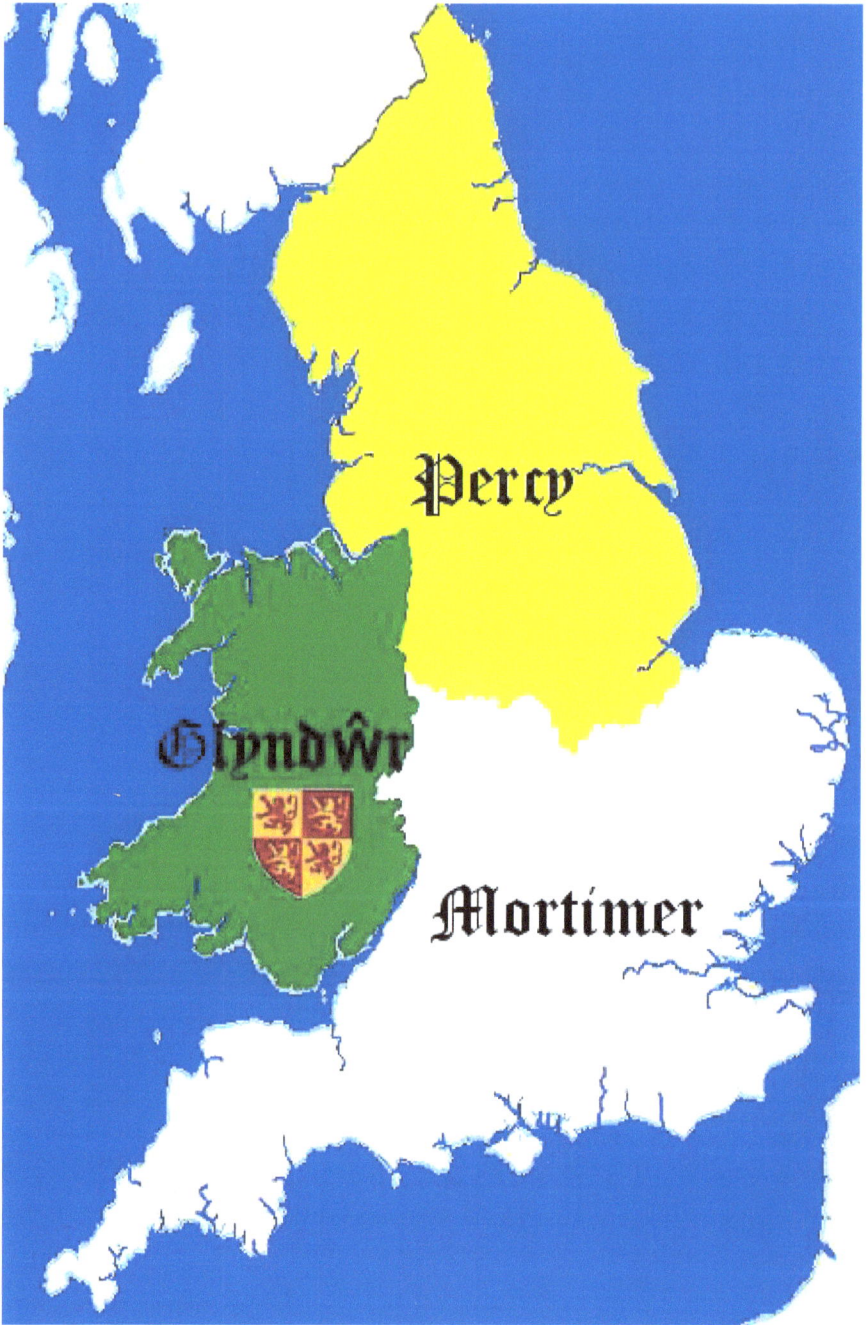

Tripartite indenture map, showing the partition of England and Wales

The Battles of Grosmont and Pwll Melyn 1405 A.D

While Owain was concluding the tripartite indenture, Rhys Gethin, Sir John Hanmer, Gruffydd (Owain's son) and Owain's brother Tudur were sent to south east Wales to reduce the last English controlled castles. The Norman castle of Grosmont guarded the Golden valley with Skenrith and White castle, strengthening the English control over the district of Abergavenny and also blocking any Welsh attempts to invade England. Both sides knew this area would be the key to winning the war in the south. Unbeknown to the Welsh, Prince Henry had bolstered up the defence of Grosmont and the vicinity, by sending a large force of archers and men-at-arms under the command of Sir John Greynder, William Newport and the Talbot brothers (John later Earl of Shrewsbury and Gilbert). On the 11th of March Rhy's men fell upon Grosmont and ransacked the town, destroying all the buildings and murdering anyone who resisted. Overconfident and laden down with booty they turned their attention towards the castle. As the Welsh settled down to besiege the fortress, Lord Talbot arrived at the scene and led a charge of his household knights. The castle's garrison opened the gates and also charged the Welsh positions. Talbot's knights hacked their way deep into the ranks of the disorganised Welsh troops. Although outnumbered, the surprise attack by the English garrison and Talbot's men forced the Welsh to flee the field of battle. News of the victory was sent to King Henry IV by his son Henry (Prince of Wales). The battle was a bloody affair and a serious defeat for Glyndŵr in the region.

Eager to regain the initiative after Rhys Gethin's defeat, Gruffydd took command of the remaining Welsh forces in the South. Believing that the main concentration of

English troops was based around Grosmont, Gruffydd decided to launch an attack on Usk castle, south of Monmouth. Henry may have had advanced warning of the plan to attack Usk, as he had re-enforced the garrison with some of his most trusted Knights including Sir Richard Grey (Baron Grey of Codnor), Sir John Greyndour, Sir John Oldcastle from Herefordshire and the Welsh squire Dafydd Gam.

Grosmont castle, Monmouthshire, Wales

The assault on the castle began in earnest; John ap Hywel (the Abbot of Llantarnam) encouraged the Welsh troops forward exclaiming that anyone who fell that day would be guaranteed a place in heaven. Using the cover of the legendary longbow men, the Welsh tried to scale the walls and beat down the gates of the fortress, but the ferocious attack on the castle was repulsed by the defenders. Then the garrison sallied out in great numbers and took the fight to Gruffydd's men. Gruffydd realised almost immediately that he had bitten off more than he could chew and ordered his men to retreat. The Welsh forded the Usk River and tried to reach the safety of the Monkswood forest. At a place called Mynydd Pwll Melyn - "Hill of the Yellow Pool" the Welsh made a final last stand. In the bloody hand to hand fighting Owain's own brother Tudor was cut down. The Abbot of Llantarnam was killed trying to flee the field and Gruffydd was overwhelmed and taken prisoner. The slaughter of the Welsh was horrendous; over 1,500 men were killed in the fighting around the forest of Monkswood and on the hill of Pwll Melyn. The chronicler Adam de Usk reported that:

"There slew fire and the edge of the sword many of them, including the Abbot of Llanternam. They crushed them without stopping, driving them through Monkswood, where Owain Glyndwr's son was taken. 300 of the Welsh captives were then beheaded near the castle".

When the body the Tudor was discovered, the English thought that had killed Glyndŵr himself. Only later did they realise that the body did not have the wart above the eye, distinguishing Owain from his brother. Some 300 unfortunate Welsh prisoners were taken back to Usk castle and then publicly beheaded. Gruffydd was quickly put in chains and dispatched to London where he was imprisoned in the dreaded Tower of London. He spend the next six years of his life as an English prisoner, finally succumbing to the plague. The battles of Grosmont and Pwll Melyn were a disaster to Glyndŵr's cause, not only had he lost the initiative in the south, but he had also lost one of his sons, his brother and some of his most able commanders and loyal warriors, including his brother in law John Hanmer.

Last through of the dice "The French invasion"

After the victories of Grosmont and Pwll Melyn, King Henry IV mustered to feudal host of England at Hereford and prepared to crush the Welsh rebellion once and for all. His plans were scuppered by a Northern rising instrumented by the Earl of Northumberland (Henry Percy), the Archbishop of York (Richard le Scrope) and Thomas Mowbray (the Earl of Norfolk). Before being able to link up with the Earl of Northumberland, Scrope and Mowbray were duped and then taken prisoner by the King's man in the north, Richard Neville (the Earl of Westmoreland). Both men were taken to York and executed on charges of treason.

The Northern rebellion had given Owain a rest bite from the threat of English invasion. However during June of 1405 A.D an English fleet sailed from Ireland and attacked the important island of Anglesey. After Beaumaris castle was recaptured by the English, Welsh resistance on Anglesey collapsed. Glyndŵr managed to score some successes in the middle march of Wales by capturing Radnor castle and laying waste to Cefnllys castle and Knighton. In August the anticipated French expedition finally landed in Pembrokeshire. Although most of the French war-horses had died of thirst during the voyage, the invasion force was indeed substantial. The 2,500 French contingent sacked the settlement of Haverfordwest, but failed to take the fortified castle. Picton castle was attacked before the French linked up with Glyndŵr's force near Tenby. Together they besieged Tenby, but an English fleet managed to break the siege and sink fourteen French ships in the bay. With no escape route from Wales for the time being, the French advanced inland with Owain onto the important town of Carmarthen. When Carmarthen castle fell to the Franco-Welsh army panic quickly spread over the border to England. Glyndŵr wanted to reduce the last English strongholds in Wales, but his French allies wanted to invade England. Owain had little choice but to agree to the French plan and march towards the border. The Franco-Welsh army ravaged the English frontier outposts and settlements. Not since before the Norman Conquest had a Welsh army raided deep into English territory.

French troops of the 15th century

Some 9 miles outside Worcester the advance was halted, when scouts brought back news that King Henry was heading towards them with the English army. Owain immediately set up defensive position on the ancient Iron Age hill fort of Woodbury Hill (known today as Owen's camp). From this position he saw the royal banners come into view on the 9th of August.

The King took up position on Abberly Hill with the objective of blocking any further advance into England. Although both armies were similar in size, neither side would commit to attacking the other's defensive position. Owain faced a serious dilemma, his French allies wanted him to take the initiative and attack the Royalist forces, but Owain knew the capability of the Welsh/English longbow. The English had won many battles particularly against the French (Crécy 1346 and Poitiers 1356 A.D) by using the longbow from a defensive position. Attacking in such circumstances would amount the military suicide. Owain was also in enemy territory, with his supply lines stretched to the maximum.

The only way to feed and sustain his army was to keep on moving, but this was impossible unless he dared risk a battle. Owain decided against an attack and instead held his position on Woodbury hill. During the next several days minor skirmishes and personal

Seal of Owain Glyndŵr, Machynlleth

challenges took place in which some 400 men were killed. After a week of stalemate Owain decided to call off the campaign and slowly retreated back over the border into Wales. The French were disgusted and although many of the foot soldiers stayed, most of the Knights and senior commanders took ship and sailed back to France. In late September the King launched an expeditionary raid into Wales to counter any Welsh plans to invade England again. Some of the English castle garrisons were relieved, but the campaign of 1405 A.D achieved little in the way of subduing the rebellion.

1406 A.D The rebellion falters

The failure to achieve a victory on the battlefield against the King's forces during the invasion of England stripped Owain of any further help from France. It also may have affected the Welsh people psychologically. Six years of bloody warfare had left the Principality ruined. The economic embargo had all but brought trade to a standstill and the yearly English campaigns had destroyed what little crops could be grown. Without an end to the war insight many started to believe in the long term Owain could not win and reconciliation was the only way forward. Prince Henry was keen to offer pardons and by doing so reduce Owain's manpower resources.

In March 1406 A.D Owain called a Parliament to gather in the small town of Pennal near Machynlleth. Glyndŵr drafted the famous Pennal letter to King Charles IV of France. The document was a last ditched effort to try and gain support from continental Europe.

Objectives of the Pennal letter:

Recognition of Wales as a separate state from England.

To establish two Universities in Wales.

The Welsh church should be independent of England with St David's Cathedral as the Archbishopric.

Depiction by Aneurin Jones of the Pennal parliament of 1406 A.D, Church of St. Peter Ad Vincula, Pennal, Wales

Only a month after the drafting of the Pennal letter the Welsh suffered another disastrous military defeat. According to the report 1000 Welshmen were slain in the encounter. Sir Edward Charleton claimed to have inflicted the heavy defeat with one of Owain's sons killed in the fighting. By the summer of 1406 A.D many Welshmen sympathetic to the cause were starting to accept Prince Henry's pardons and switch sides. According to Adam of Usk, the Welsh Crusading knight Dafydd ab ieuan Goch was sent by the King of France on Owain's behalf, on a secret mission to Scotland. He objective was to try and bring Scotland into the war, forcing Henry to fight on three fronts. Unfortunately Dafydd's ship was boarded by English sailors before it could reach Scottish waters. On discovering letters and the identity of their prisoner the English captain sent Dafydd to London where he was thrown into the Tower of London. In November, 2000 Welsh rebels were fined for their involvement in the revolt and then pardoned. Owain tried to regain the initiative by raiding the English border, the great castle of Rhuddlan was attacked and Glyndŵr's men ravaged to border from Chester in the north of Hereford in the south. Over 50 churches were reported to have been destroyed by the Welsh raiders.

1407 A.D The fall of resistance, Aberystwyth castle

Prince Henry decided to lead the English "Chevauchee" of 1407 A.D due to his father's poor health. At Hereford the Prince ordered carpenters to cut down trees in the forest of Dean for the construction of siege engines. Instead of the annual raid into Wales, Prince Henry had decided to launch an attack on Owain's impregnable power base of Aberystwyth castle. Six cannons from the newly formed Royal artillery train were dispatched from Pontefract castle in Yorkshire to help reduce the resistance of the Welsh. The Prince set out into Wales with some of the most experienced battle hardened veterans of the war including Richard Beauchamp (the Earl of Warwick), Sir John Oldcastle, Baron Audley and the Duke of York. As the royal army advanced deep into South Wales Thomas, Lord of Carew led the Pembrokeshire militia out and joined forces with the Prince's army. In the face of overwhelming odds Welsh resistance melted away into the hills and forests. By late summer, the Prince's forces laid siege to the great fortress. The siege of Aberystwyth castle was the first time cannon and gunpowder were used against a castle on British soil. A notable fatality was William Gwyn ap Rhys Llwyd of Cydweli. The bombards pounded Aberystwyth's walls and even the huge 5,000 pound gun called the "Messager" was used in the siege, the latter was destroyed by an accidental discharge along with its crew. With Aberystwyth cut off from both sea and land, it was only a matter of time before the garrison would either surrender or be overwhelmed. In late September the castle's commander Rhys Du asked for a truce in which the castle would be handed over to the English on all Saints day (1st of November). The English commander Sir Richard Courtenay agreed and Rhys was allowed to leave the siege and report the news to his master Owain Glyndŵr. Owain was in the heart of Gwynedd when Rhys came before him to tell him the developments from Aberystwyth. Owain flew into a rage and threatened Rhys on pain of death unless he reneged on his promise with the English. Owain marched south with several hundred troops to bolster up the garrison of Aberystwyth. They met no resistance as the English had already retreated to their winter quarters, expecting the castle to surrender on the promised date.

The winter of 1407-1408 A.D

In November dreadful news arrived from France. King Charles VI bouts of madness had led to a power struggle between John the Fearless, the Duke of Burgundy (Charles cousin) and Louis of Orléans (Charles VI brother) for control of the realm of France. On the 23rd of November 1407 A.D Louis was assassinated by the Duke's men in the streets of Paris. Louis' murder caused a civil war and blood feud between the Burgundians and Armagnac's (supporters of the dead Louis and the French Royal family). Louis had been a long advocate against any reconciliation with England and his death proved a hammer blow to Owain who desperately needed French troops and support against England. The Earl of Northumberland, Thomas Bardolf and the Bishop of Bangor left the French court and returned to Scotland to try and raise an army to invade England.

In February the rebels crossed the border, but were defeated at the battle of Bramham Moor near Wetherby by the Sheriff of York (Sir Thomas Rokeby). Both Henry Percy and Bardolf were killed in the fighting, but the Bishop of Bangor was spared because he was captured wearing his religious vestments. The rebel heads and corpses were sent to London, Lincoln and York as a warning to any would-be traitors.

As the snow started to fall in the winter on 1407-08 Wales became a cold and desolate country. The harsh winter forced both sides to abandon military operations and wait until spring to re-prosecute the war. Owain knew after the defeat of the Northern rebels and the death of his ally the Duke de Orleans that his dream of an independent Wales was slipping from his grasp. When the snow and ice thwarted in the spring of 1408 A.D Owain sent ambassadors to France asking for urgent assistance. Prince Henry invaded Wales and immediately re-commenced the siege of Aberystwyth.

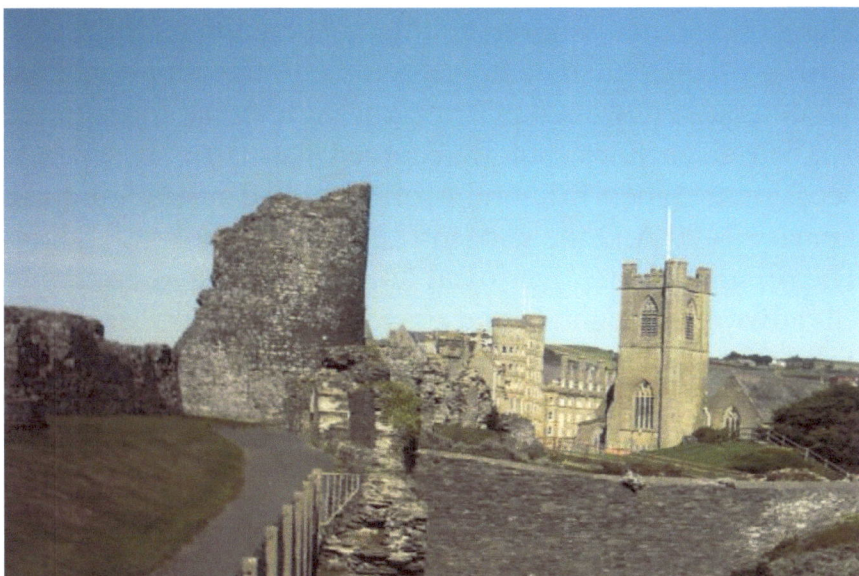

The ruins of the once mighty Aberystwyth castle

In order to put further pressure on the rebels he sent Gilbert and John Talbot north to besiege Owain's royal residence of Harlech castle. By besieging Harlech, Prince Henry would in effect be cutting off Aberystwyth from any relief attempts from Glyndŵr in Snowdonia. The plan worked perfectly and although one of Owain's captains Rhys ap Gruffydd vowed he would not allow the castle to fall, by September of 1408 A.D the rest of the Welsh garrison could endure no more. Most of the Welsh soldiers escaped under the cover of nightfall and took ship across Cardigan Bay towards Snowdonia. On the 12th of September Maredudd ab Owain (Rhys Ddu's son in law) was handed over as a hostage, allowing the remaining garrison to leave the castle unmolested.

The siege of Harlech 1408-1409 A.D

After the surrender of Aberystwyth castle Prince Henry turned his full attention to Harlech. Overseeing the Castle's defence was Sir Edmund Mortimer. Owain's wife Margaret and her children huddled behind the mighty stone walls as the English cannons pounded huge stone balls at the defences. Owain desperately tried to break through the English siege lines, but was forced back to two separate occasions. When Edmund Mortimer died of starvation in January 1409 A.D the garrison surrendered to Lord Talbot. The English were overjoyed to have captured Margaret Glyndŵr, her daughters and grandson Lionel De Mortimer. Talbot immediately sent the valuable prisoners under a heavily armed escort to London. Once in the English capital they were imprisoned in the Tower of London facing a bleak future in Royal confinement.
Owain was distraught when he found out the news from Harlech, only his son Maredudd could comfort his father in his hour of need. The fall of Harlech signaled the end of

the Welsh dream to be free from English oppression. From that moment onwards Owain Glyndŵr became a fugitive and a hunted man in his own country.

The last raid into England 1409 A.D

Filled with uncontrollable rage, Owain gathered together the last of his loyal band of supporters and rode out towards the English border for one final destructive raid. The Welsh laid waste to the English settlements between Oswestry and Shrewsbury. Farms were razed to the ground with fire and livestock slaughtered as Owain sought revenge for the capture of his wife and family. Glyndŵr's men left a trail of destruction in their wake. As the English countryside burned, the local nobility were galvanised into action.

Near Welshpool Glyndŵr's raiding party was ambushed and then routed by the English Marcher forces. The Welsh troops and knights were butchered in the vicious combat. Owain's cousin Rhys ap Tudor (the mastermind behind the capture of Conwy castle in 1401 A.D) was captured along with Philip Scudamore and Rhys Ddu the defender of Aberystwyth castle. Rhys Ddu was sent to London to face a gruesome execution, while both Tudor and Scudamore were beheaded in Shrewsbury and Chester to appease the English crowds. After the death of Tudor there was a minor uprising on Anglesey, but this was swiftly put down by English re-enforcements sent to the island to restore order.

Owain was extremely lucky not to have been captured or killed in the raid. He retreated back into Wales never to launch a raid into England again. Instead he retreated to the mountain stronghold's of Snowdonia and Powys where he remained free from English attempts to capture him.

Night attack during the last raid of 1409 A.D

The fugitive and disappearance 1410 – 14 ? A.D

After the last raid of 1409 A.D Glyndŵr remained at large to continue a guerilla war against the English and their Welsh supporters. Owain roamed Wales encouraging his people never to accept English rule. In 1412 A.D Glyndŵr managed to capture the Welsh traitor Dafydd Gam (crooked David). Owain decided to ransom Gam on the condition that he swear never to bear arms against him again. As soon as Gam was released he betrayed his oath and told the English of Glyndŵr's whereabouts. Owain managed to evade capture and descended on Brecon, burning Gam's house and farm to the ground.

During the winter of 1413 A.D Owain received the news that his daughter Catrin Mortimer and her children had all died in the Tower of London. It is not recorded what happened to his wife Margaret, but the death of his children and grand children must have caused deep sorrow. Although there is no evidence that they were murdered, the Mortimer claim to the throne would have certainly made them possible rivals to King Henry V.

In 1414 A.D the Earl of Arundel took the surrender of over 500 rebels at Bala in North Wales, they were fined and then pardoned as part of Prince Henry's (Now King Henry V) policy of reconciliation towards the Welsh. Even as late as 1415 A.D Owain's ambassadors were still active in France trying to get French support to re-activate the war. When the Southampton plot to murder King Henry V and replace him with Edmund Mortimer (the Earl of March and Richard II heir) was uncovered Glyndŵr's hopes of toppling the Lancastrian King from power was finally at an end. King Henry V even sent Lord Talbot into Wales to offer a pardon to Owain and his loyal followers. No response was fore coming and Glyndŵr may still have been reeling from the death his relatives in the Tower of London.

Owain simply disappeared and unlike Scotland's William Wallace "Braveheart" and the French heroine Joan d'Arc the English were unable to capture Glyndŵr. According to Adam of Usk:

"Owain Glyndwr died four years after he laid hidden from the King. He was buried by his supporters, but on the discovery of his burial place he was re-inurned in a secret grave. His body so bestowed so noone would find it".

There are many legends and theories about the fate of Owain Glyndŵr. One story says that Owain spent his last days taking refuge and visiting his surviving daughters Alice and Margaret at Monnington court and Kentchurch Castle (home of the Scudamore family since the Norman invasion). A horse was always saddled for him day and night incase he needed to make a quick getaway, but like King Arthur before him we may never know the exact truth of how Owain died or where he is buried.

Owain's son Maredudd ap Owain Glyndŵr kept fighting the English until 1421 A.D when he finally accepted a pardon from the English crown. Even after Maredudd's pardon Welsh patriots such as Owain's son in law Philip ap Rhys refused to surrender. Well into the next century the Gwylliad Cochion Mawddwy (the Red haired bandits of Mawddwy terrorised parts of mid Wales and flaunted Royal authority.

Owain Glyndŵr is Wales' "Braveheart"; his is a story of loyalty, defending Welsh culture, humility, courage, victory, defeat and finally a mysterious disappearance. Had his revolt succeeded, then the British Isles we know of today may well be very different indeed. He will always be regarded as Wales' greatest patriot and a man who united his country against oppression for freedom and independence.

> **"Long must the island Monarch roam,**
> **The noble heart and the mighty land;**
> **But we shall bear him proudly home**
> **To his father's mountain home"**

Also from the author:

INTO THE DRAGON'S LAIR
"The Norman Conquest of Wales and the Marches"
1066-1283 A.D

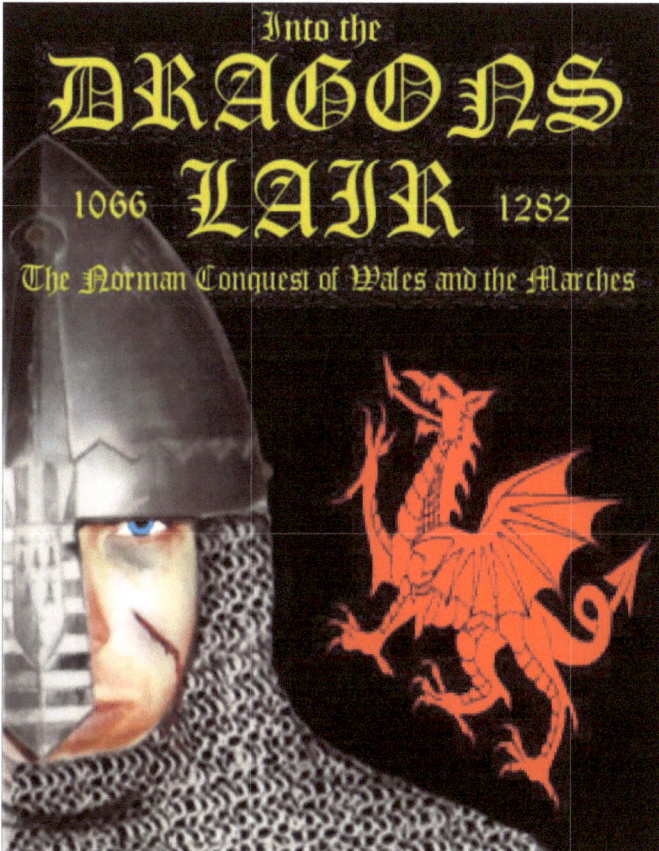

www.ingramcontent.com/pod-product-compliance
Lightning Source LLC
LaVergne TN
LVHW010025070426
835509LV00001B/9